RAVENSWOOD

RICHARD RYAN

RAVENSWOOD

THE DOLMEN PRESS

Set in Baskerville type and printed and published
in the Republic of Ireland at the Dolmen Press,
North Richmond Street, Dublin 1.
SBN 85105 255 x

First published 1973

Distributed outside Ireland, except
in the U.S.A. and in Canada
by Oxford University Press

General distributors in the U.S.A. and in Canada
Humanities Press Inc.,
450 Park Avenue South,
New York, N.Y. 10016

CONTENTS

Acknowledgement is due to the editors of:

Aquarius; Atlantis; Caret; Choice; The Dublin Magazine; The Faber Book of Irish Verse; Hibernia; The Humanist; The Irish Times; The Malahat Review; The Nation; Poetry: Introduction 2 (Faber & Faber); *Soundings '72; The Spectator; The Times Literary Supplement.*

From My Lai the Thunder Went West was printed in a limited edition by the Dolmen Press, Dublin (July, 1970).

Some of these poems were broadcast on B.B.C. Radio Three (Great Britain), and National Public Radio (United States).

The Maid in the Moor and *Wulf and Eadwacer* are versions from the Middle and Old English respectively.

Dream in a dream the heavy soul somewhere
struck suddenly & dark down to its knees.
A griffin sighs off in the orphic air.

JOHN BERRYMAN

GOING

The west drifts, a cathedral of air.

Through all the neat villages
Gathered under their stones, bells
Are bonging,
Customary and weird as bird-song.

From the bright and alive hearts of hedgerows
And the high dusty corners of barns
Something is beginning to gather
Up the light in handfuls now

While the villages drift,
Dreaming of light, over the edge of the world.

The roads are astray in the woods.
Through the darkest places
Fireflies are staggering, blundering
Into tree-shapes and sinking,
Their cracked antennae uselessly whirling

As now, singly,
The cities are lifting away,
They are floating like constellations slowly,
Keeping together and speaking of direction.

Far to the west of our world
Blood will be journeying tonight,
Windows swaying softly over dark waters.

NIGHTFALL
for Charles McCafferty

Men worry, or
don't, and live on
in the intricate canyon

of stone and smoke
their city is, flashing
its morse to the sun

like a retarded man
attempting to speak; and
thus Autumn passed away

until the fish were locked
into the lakes and
in the thin bones of stones

and trees something
finally gave up.
The last thrush went into

the ground and the sun
skimming low over the hills
where odd knots of cloud

were gathering, saw
it had nowhere to go
anymore and fell to pieces

in a snow field as night
fell, and the first star
guttered quickly over

their city where behind
glass the men almost heard
something, and glanced briefly

into the dark beyond knowing,
beyond knowing where or why
they worry and live on, or don't.

ELM

Like thoughts they began to slip
nightly into the high dark cave of his head
until there were rows and rows of them

like furry black fruit
hanging by their toes along the thin veins
of the branches in the dark

where he hardly noticed them
unless from time to time one slipped
and fell with a shriek

to wake the dead from where they sleep
but he drank the rain to live
and never dreamed that they too

ate to live until one night in winter
he awoke with his head in the moon
hearing them where they flew and flew

slipping like leaves to the ground
all their hearts
through branches where leaves once were.

FLESH AND BONE

A shape there, in the dark? But a veil
Whirrs by again to block and madden sight;
Flesh-shapes writhe in its fantastic light
Till heart or will, or both, must seem to fail.

Once, for once there were clear nights, I could
Pick their faint truths from stars, reduce to bone
All flesh; kept my tools clean, and was alone.
Now vicious winter ploughs the skies to mud

And all roads are treacherous; searching
For bone I had piled the flesh in heaps, nor
Counted how it rose up from the floor
Till now all sight is blocked by flesh twitching.

I might have stopped long since were not my
Tools the oldest known to surgery.

WINTER IN MINNEAPOLIS
for Eóin McKiernan

From my high window I can watch
the freeways coiling on their strange
stilts to where the city glows
through rain like a new planet.

Tonight the radio speaks
of snow and in the waste plots
below trees stiffen,
frost wrinkles the pools.

Through high dark air
the apartment buildings,
like computer panels, begin
again to transmit their faint signals —

for they are there now, freed one and all
from the far windy towns, the thin
bright girls compounded of heat,
movement, and a few portable needs.

But I have no calls to make tonight,
for we are all strangers here
who have only the night to share —
stereos, soft lights, and small alarm clocks:

of our photograph albums, our far
towns, and our silences we do not speak;
wisely we have learned to respect
the locked door and unanswered telephone.

I turn from my window and pause a moment
in darkness. My bed and desk
barely visible, clean paper
waits in its neat circle of light. . . .

I wait; and slowly they appear, singly,
like apparitions. They stand all round me,
on metal bridges and in the wet streets,
their long hair blowing and they will not go.

MIKE,

the truth of your final, desperate act
is faltering slowly, helplessly, as wind
and flurries of sudden snow
circle in over the dead lakes.

And this small Minnesota town
I have never seen before, nor will again,
stumbles slowly to a halt
as its barns, rusted railway sheds

and a last abandoned motel yield
silently to the snow-filled fields,
staggering fences, and a ghostly cluster
of pines and sunk crosses

where we assemble, a thick huddle
of family and friends ringing the narrow grave
and the blunt priest doing his best,
the wind whipping his words away, the cold

quick as a fist reaching for us too. . . .
But we finish it and return, shivering
to cars or the hot bars, our breath pluming,
life drifting back into stiff limbs

until slowly, casually as snow
a further truth drifts in
and I stare where, with utter simplicity,
the snow is gathering steadily around us all.

BRIGHT SAILS
in memory of John Berryman

I

Blind harper, blind
fiddler, blind poet;
old hold-alls stuffed

with rags and ragged
dreams, petty session
held in ditch and shebeen.

The wise threw bright sails
to the wind and dropped
dead in their dreams

between candle and quill,
rats at them.

II

Like truth, over
the horizons they stumble now,

all our confused galleons
staggering in tempest,
collapsing under the weight

of their priceless cargoes;
on the rocks they flounder
toward, the girls glitter

the gifts of their bodies
opening like wounds, while again
on a far horizon the dawn sails by

like a world that works,
brown men singing in its rigging,

a golden fleet forever sailing the wrong way.

THE LAKE OF THE WOODS
for Chester Anderson

Winter began with
The birches turning to glass
And the wild geese

Over the lake nightly,
Evacuating in their loud squadrons.
For weeks still there

Were roads, light
And the repeating moons; but
Slowly, through the sunk woods

Snow is climbing toward
The cabins now and
Twice already our cemetery

Has opened its
Mouth and closed it again.
Nothing lives in the woods

Any longer, only
A crumbling moon and the stars
Above the lake

Collapsing, one by one.
It is getting worse, and
We will survive

As we are able: out
On the lake a man has chopped
A hole in the ice

To fish through; his
Son is snapping twigs from
The pines, it

Sounds like pistols,
but suddenly there is a fish on the ice.
Daily it worsens

But somehow they know,
The fish and the trees
And the men, that it is temporary,

That some bright
Morning the geese will return
Singing down the

Runways of sunlight and lake water.
We are sure.
Or we have no memory,

Any of us, of the ice
Like an iron giant
Stalking the earth, that

Deep beneath the
Snow, the buried bottles
And the wrecked boots, beyond

All further thaw
A lost world of lizards
And leaves lies frozen in stone.

EL DORADO

Under a swaying
crucifix cursing,
bitten by flies,

an army is slicing
its way through
flowers as the

hummingbird darts
away and the snake
melts back into

its hot pools.
Far above, on
the cool roof

of the world,
the temples glitter
through cloud and

tall priests chant
urgently under their
great god of gold.

But their prayers
are unheard as, gold
gleaming in their

fevered eyes, the
white strangers begin
to close in, and

briefly their tall
cross catches the
last of the light —

twin gods conversing —
before yet another
world sinks, dying

under that iron cross.
Soldiers of Christ
they ransack the

buildings for women
and gold, but above
them the white condor

lifts, its great wings
stained with the blood
of the dying sun, to

drift slowly away.

FROM MY LAI
THE THUNDER WENT WEST

and it all died down
to an underground
tapping and then that,
too, stopped dead.

In cornfield, wheat
field, a black
sheet of earth
was drawn neatly

across the seed
they planted.
And the fields turn
daily to the sun.

Come high Summer
and the first shoots
will appear, puzzling
the sun as, growing

through earth, growing
through grass, the
human crop they have sown —
child bone, wife

bone, man
bone will stand
wavering in the pale fields:
the silent, eye-

less army will
march west through
Autumn and Europe
until, streaked

with December rain
they will stand in
New York and Texas;
as the lights click

out across America
they will fence in
the houses, tapping
on window, tapping

on door. Till
dawn, then rain only:
from sea to sea drifting,
drops of bright ruby.

THE MAID IN THE MOOR

A maid in the dark moor lay,
   In the moor wide and deep,
A sennight full, a sennight long
The maid in the moor lay,
   In the moor wide and deep
Seven nights long, and a day.

Ah, but she ate well —
   But what was her meat? — tell.
The primerole and the —
The primerole and —
Ah, but she ate well,
   But what did she eat? —
The primerole and the violet.

Ay, and she drank well,
   But what could she drink? — tell !
The chil'st water from the spring well.

Bright bricks for her bower,
   From what came her bower? —
Alas, the red rose and the lily flower.

ALL GONE

Gone the sad, silly
Dreams of forever —

And gone the other
Dark forms we dreamed

To shape once deep
In their nests

Of blood, they trail
Through mist now

Between us where
We move, they float

Forever beyond life
Or death through

The dark spaces
We will never reach —

They are breathless
And perfect now

As the pale hollow
Pod of this moon

Slipping free at
Last from the claw

Of these bright
Dying branches of bone.

THEN LET US SHARE ALL, MY LOVE

The last of the light
left your small room;
the cooker began to tick
and the television grew legs.

I lifted my hand and
you rose. I opened my secret
trap-door in the floor and a door
creaked open behind your eyes.

You descended the damp steps
most beautifully, but entered
a cul-de-sac of stone that ended
in pale ribs and a skull, and claws.

Or deeper, where something
slithered suddenly out of the darkness
and tore off an offering,
its twitching head, begging exchange with you. . . .

And down you fled
through the shrieking halls
to where an old man raved in the flare
of his ruby eyes, his furious chisel

splitting the stone
that is the heart of the world.
And scattered there among the skulls
diamonds, their tears.

WULF AND EADWACER

This gang who protect me
    can't wait to get at him:
a bright welcome he'll feel
    when their blades bite into him!

Hope fades for us now

Wulf on one island,
    I stuck on another,
seas swamping the reeds
    where armed men move:
their hooked eyes
    are on the horizons,
their hopes are high.

Hope fades for us now

By the fire in wet
    weather when I thought
of your touch, the
    storms that broke in me!
My body wept after
    one of these ruffians
forced me, but
    Wulf, at the time
I didn't know the difference.

Wulf, Wulf,
    my bones show, but
it's your absence
    has brought me to this;
I take no heed
    of food I don't need.

Hopeless here, do
    you hear, Eadwacer?
He'll slink to the
    wood, escape us all.

Easily stopped what
    had hardly started,
our song together.

GIRL, WATERFALL

The river a lizard on fire
Screaming and lashing its tail!

Till I fell
Through a hole in the air
Away down below a place where
Light and dark meet and are not either.

Head a moon now,
Light leaking out all over.
I am light slipping into the skin of the river,
I am coming apart
Softly, my skin
Flying slowly in all directions. . . .

And the rocks in my waters now, plunging
And drowning, their thin skins all melting away

Oh, the rocks!

I am nowhere

TERMINAL

The mist lifted suddenly,
It was the edge of the world.

We dream and leave, my love.

Because darkness through
Green fields slipping, because the fields of flowers.

Because the lie that is hid in the heart of the world.

BALL-GAME

In his cunning he brought her puppies
and the choicest of fruits. He
wriggled and dripped at her delight.

With love he pumped her up
until a skin moon her tummy,
tiny hearts chirping behind her walls.

She cooked cleaned scrubbed wiped
it was lovely, their
babies bounced round them like balls.

Forever and ever and ever
it was, a ball-game and dinner out,
never was there anything like it;

a Sunday it was,
sunny on the front porch
dropped down he did, of a sudden,

watch-springs everywhere.
Who'd have thought and him so nice,
and baby five saying look at daddy.

FUNCTION

Here again, those
Signals from below,
All else replaced
The fierce pulse
Rising to beat mind
Down. And I obey,
Flesh seeking flesh,
Reduced to function
By demand from below
The floor of life, that
Swirling liquid world
Where the unborn swarm.

PROCESS

A child with parents once and wild
in the living woods, knew secrets
in leaves where with stopped heart
he stared at the dark eggs tick
or stood silent once among streams
in a river of light.

And then the plans, where with grave eyes
he knelt among dying whispers, broken guns,
was a strider of the red sunsets
or home on the range, in love with his wife
and his head of pure silver,
a grower of apples and sons.

It was all there,
and birds fly south in winter.
And one year they took
his apples with them and
his parents and the long red plains,
and down from his blue eyes

the dreams dropped like leaves
in the suddenly murdered woods,
and he turned to himself
and cried aloud, for look
where all his shining future crept,
that slow stream drying in the hot canyons.

IRELAND

That ragged
leaking raft held
between sea and sea

its long
forgotten cable melting
into deeper darkness where,

at the root
of it, the slow
sea circles and chews.

Nightly the dark-
ness lands like hands
to mine downward, springing

tiny leaks
till dawn finds
field is bog, bog lake.

MOHER

The earth is
round all
right, but here

earth ends, thick
tongues of mist
licking the ledge.

A hiss — the
sea breathing?
That crying is not birds. . . .

Thrown up screaming,
a chough, its claws
and beak blazing —

it grabs at light,
then topples shrieking
down out of the world.

RAVENSWOOD

The light shrank
back and Ravenswood
locked us in.

Armed to fight
men, our hearts stalled
where ravens dangled

dead. Why prize
what's already lost?
We left the wood's

shelter, were found
and died, red iron
skirling in our throats.

*   *   *

Field, booty won,
the victors wiped their knives
and praised the plot

but who would
enter Ravenswood
to cut the ravens down?

I AM EARTH

Bells ringing,
All our bright
Flags flying,

Six busy nuns
At my helm, I
Am the great ageing

Zeppelin of the
World, secure in
My bubble of foul

Air and sailing
Finally home
Now, my marvellous

Radios dwindling
To a last
Crackle of static

Speaking of love,
Disasters, and
The price of green

Money. We lost
Forty-seven thousand
Humans, many

Trees and a tractor
Last week R.I.P.,
The primroses are

Thriving. Up
Front, in com-
Partment XI29B, a

Farmyard next door
To the Brahms
Concert, our valuable

Last European long-
Head is praying
Noisily to himself

Watch his hens circle
Him, nodding vigorously
To each other or

To nobody and
Banging their red
Heads on my stones.

SPACE-WALK

The metal skin
of the mother ship

parts briefly as
a tiny glimmering human

squeezes through to
drift soundlessly away

the umbilical cord
a line of light curling

to a brief
gathering of light

within true darkness
where all weights

slide away and dis-
appear until the cold

cord stiffens
suddenly to haul him

back and the wall
slides open again.

ROOF-PRINCIPLE

Some imagined giant
Strider of galaxies
That we say cannot be,
Become. Lift any stone
And there the living
On the floors of all
Worlds in terror teem
(Scuttle of brains,
Halved hairs of claws
Hoisting pale eggs) —
A living liquid pour-
Ing back through
Crack and tiny pore
To deeper earth where
A roof of darkness
Can hold up once more.

GALAXY

faint
   in deep space,
      immense as a brain.

down
   through the thought-
      shaft it drifts, a wale

of light to
   which the retina
      opens and is entered

time and
   space dis-
      appearing as the mind

recedes
   to a soundless
      flickering somewhere

deeper
   than consciousness
      where, permanent as

change
   a whorl of light
      rides, wheeling in darkness

MIDNIGHT

No sound but snow
falling, the sunken city

of the world drifting
silently under its crosses.

In far darkness
a siren begins to moan

softly, for this
is the world of the living

and everywhere here
punctual odd clocks are

whirring and striking.
Yes, tonight again it seems

I must climb the dark
spidery stair and again

at the top wait
shivering, staring at nothing.

Thus to return
as now, knowing nothing,

blind with belief
as a dream of winter roses

to find you waiting
in the simple firelight

soundlessly opening
your skin, bringing me in.

A PRAYER

Against rain and shrill
Siren, against night —

(*I do not know this world
nor will come here again*)

Spell, against that other dark
World where shadows are

(*a shipwreck in the sky
I have dreamed it again*)

Rummaging in the dumps and
Praying to their own dark

(*dark air breathes in the
curtains, enters this frail*)

Shadow, lives stopping and
Starting, let us pray

(*arrangement, your life and mine,
this room compounded of love only*)

No answer because no question,
A groping only, darkness

(*this dark bed where my hunger
moves in you goodbye, goodbye*)

Where we may in time learn
How to love and fall down.

RETURN

As through the dark
Fluid of a dream

Shoals of light
And life spurt and

Disappear again into
Sunk pools, dark

Eddying nets of flesh,
A tangle of odours and

Taste on the brink
Of its being so fragile

In the living darkness
It inhabits as not to exist

At all, or simply
And completely as belief

Itself, a dream of dark waters
Beyond life or death

Were it not for these odd
Sudden tremors I do not cause,

These sudden splinters
Of light, this tearing

Exquisite as pain telling me
Now, and now, and now, that I believe.